SilverTip

Cells

by Ruth Owen

Consultant: Jordan Stoleru
Science Educator

BEARPORT
PUBLISHING

Minneapolis, Minnesota

Credits

Cover and title page, © ileana_bt/Adobe Stock; 5, © Maridav/Shutterstock; 7T, © DejaVuDesigns/Shutterstock; 7B, © Ye.Maltsev/Shutterstock; 9, © brgfx/Shutterstock; 11T, © Choksawatdikorn/Shutterstock; 11M, © Pansfun Images/Shutterstock; 11B, © Pansfun Images/Shutterstock; 13, © Ldarin/Shutterstock; 15, © Pasotteo/Shutterstock; 17, © GraphicsRF.com/Shutterstock; 18 © otello-stpdc/Shutterstock; 19, © kuehdi/Shutterstock; 21, © Designua/Shutterstock; 23, © Aldona Griskeviciene/Shutterstock; 25, © Volodymyr Burdiak/Shutterstock; 27, © Prostock-studio/Shutterstock; and 28, © Designua/Shutterstock.

Bearport Publishing Company Product Development Team

President: Jen Jenson; Director of Product Development: Spencer Brinker; Managing Editor: Allison Juda; Associate Editor: Naomi Reich; Associate Editor: Tiana Tran; Senior Designer: Colin O'Dea; Associate Designer: Elena Klinkner; Associate Designer: Kayla Eggert; Product Development Specialist: Anita Stasson

Library of Congress Cataloging-in-Publication Data is available at www.loc.gov or upon request from the publisher.

ISBN: 979-8-88822-038-2 (hardcover)
ISBN: 979-8-88822-230-0 (paperback)
ISBN: 979-8-88822-353-6 (ebook)

For more information, write to Bearport Publishing, 5357 Penn Avenue South, Minneapolis, MN 55419.

Contents

Cells, Cells Everywhere

Look at a human body. Stare straight at a tree. They may seem very different. But zoom in closer than the human eye can see. They actually have a lot in common. From a person's bones and skin to a tree's bark and leaves, all living things are made of many tiny cells.

A single cell is very small. Many of them come together to make something you can actually see. There are trillions of cells in a human body. A tree leaf can have about 30 million cells.

Building Life

Cells are often called the building blocks of life. They are the smallest living parts of anything that was or is alive.

Some living things are a single cell. These are called **unicellular.** Many living things are **multicellular.** They are made of many cells grouped together.

People and other animals are multicellular. Plants are, too. What living things are unicellular? Some fungi are made of only one cell. So are the germs that can make us sick.

Up Close with Animal Cells

The cells in animals and plants are different. An animal cell has an outer layer called a cell **membrane.** Inside the membrane, there is a thick liquid called **cytoplasm** (SYE-tuh-*plaz*-uhm). A single **nucleus** and many small **mitochondria** (*mye*-tuh-KAHN-dree-uh) float in the cytoplasm.

The cell membrane keeps the cell together. It's also a little bit like a guard. It lets in the things a cell needs to be healthy. It keeps out things that could be bad for the cell.

An Animal Cell

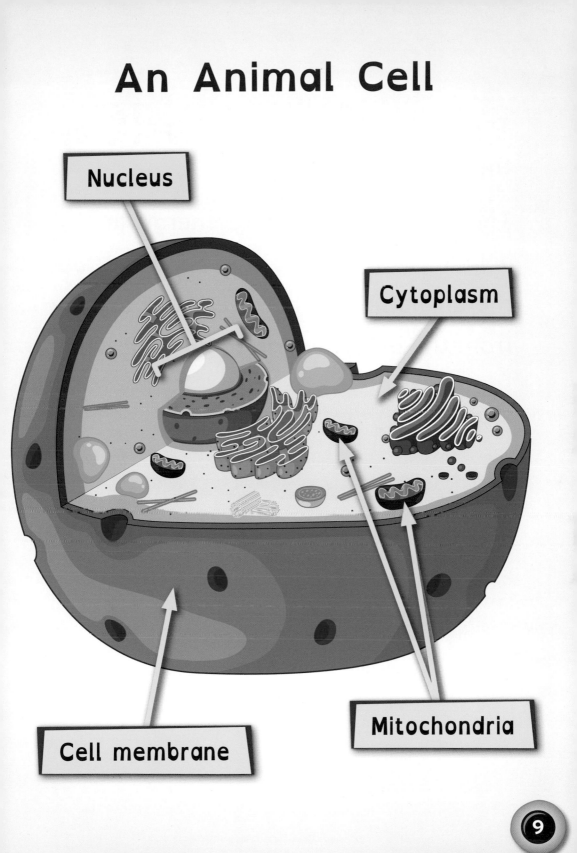

Nucleus

Cytoplasm

Cell membrane

Mitochondria

The nucleus is like a cell's brain. It tells the cell what to do.

The mitochondria create energy. In animal cells, they do this using the food the animals eat. Then, cells use energy from the mitochondria to do their work.

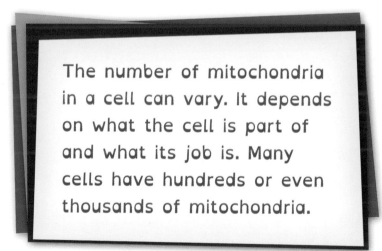

The number of mitochondria in a cell can vary. It depends on what the cell is part of and what its job is. Many cells have hundreds or even thousands of mitochondria.

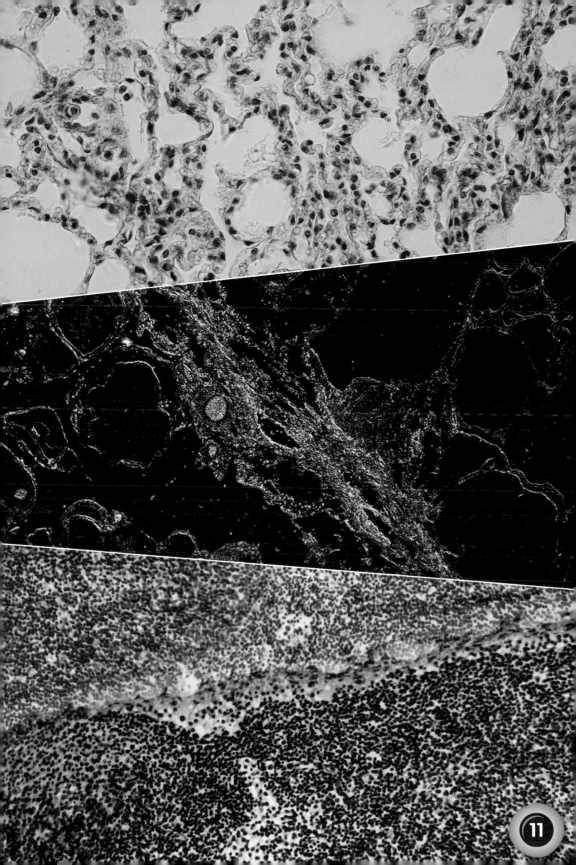

Plant Cells in Action

A plant cell also has a membrane, cytoplasm, a nucleus, and mitochondria. In addition, it has a strong cell wall.

There is a space within the cell that is called a **vacuole** (VAK-yoo-wohl). Vacuoles are small in animal cells. But they can take up most of the space inside a plant cell.

Animal cells can be soft and squishy. Often, they do not have a set shape. Plant cells are usually more square or rectangular. The solid cell wall gives them this shape.

A Plant Cell

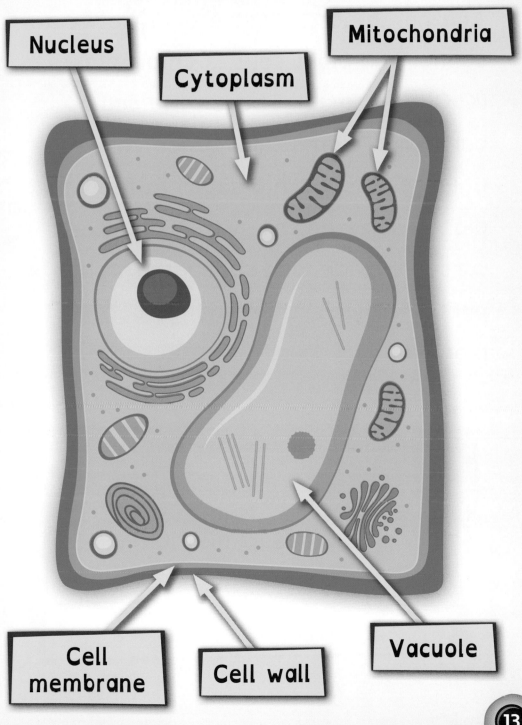

Nucleus

Cytoplasm

Mitochondria

Cell membrane

Cell wall

Vacuole

Another important difference between animal and plant cells is **chloroplasts** (KLOR-uh-*plasts*). These little cell parts give plants their green color. Chloroplasts make a sugar to feed plants. They do this with just water, carbon dioxide, and sunlight. Through photosynthesis, these things become plant food.

In plant cells, mitochondria team up with chloroplasts. Plant food is made by the chloroplasts. Then, it is turned into energy by the mitochondria. The energy lets plant cells do work, such as growing new leaves.

Many chloroplasts may be found in a single plant cell.

Cells at Work

A multicellular animal or plant has many different kinds of cells. Similar cells group together. For example, there are special cells that make up a human heart. Among these, there are different kinds, too. They help with different jobs. Cells may help things grow, repair, or stay healthy.

If you get a cut, different cells spring into action. Some blood cells kill anything bad that comes in through the cut. Skin cells and another kind of blood cells close up the injury.

There are many kinds of cells in a human body.

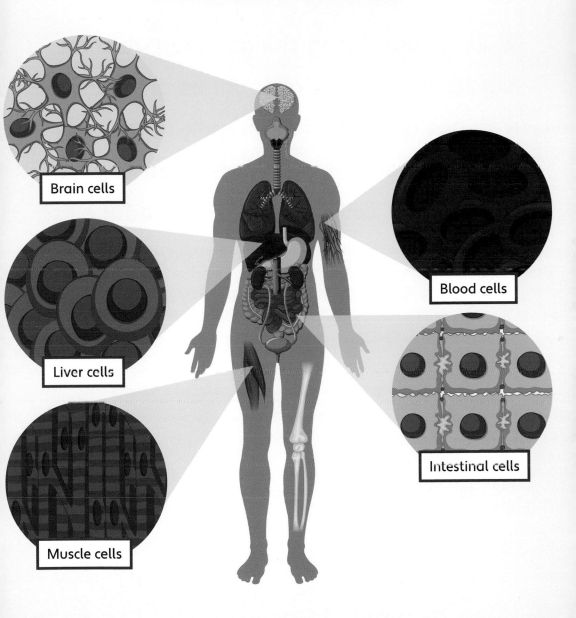

Brain cells

Blood cells

Liver cells

Intestinal cells

Muscle cells

One Becomes Two

Multicellular living things often get bigger over time. Your bones grow as you get older. A tree's trunk does, too. To get bigger, living things need to make more cells. So, cells **reproduce**. They make copies of themselves. This happens through **mitosis** (mye-TOH-sis), or cell division.

When a person or other animal breaks a bone, special bone cells start to reproduce. These cells have a job. They join the two pieces of broken bone back together.

How does a single cell become two new cells? First, the cell makes a copy of all the information in its nucleus. Then, it goes through mitosis. The cell splits in two. Both of these cells get a copy of the information that was in the original. They will go on to do the same job.

During mitosis, one cell splits in two. Then, each of those cells breaks apart as well. That makes four cells total. This can keep going to make many more cells from the same first cell.

Mitosis in Action

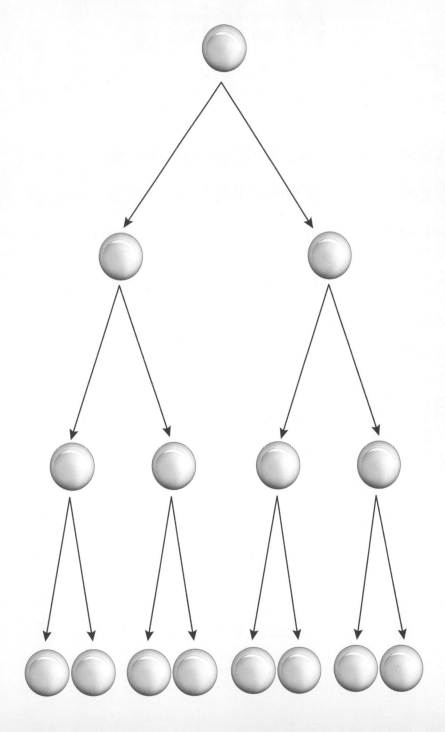

Making Something New

Mitosis can help things grow. But how do cells make new life? Most animals and many plants have some cells that go through **meiosis** (mye-OH-sis). During meiosis, a special parent cell divides in two. Then, the two cells divide to make four new kinds of cells.

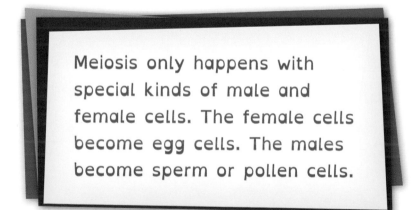

Meiosis only happens with special kinds of male and female cells. The female cells become egg cells. The males become sperm or pollen cells.

Meiosis in Action

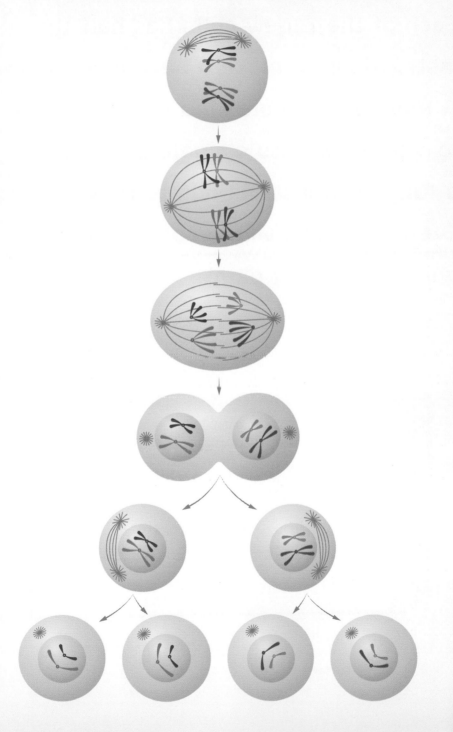

Each of these new cells has half the instructions to make a new living thing. A male and female kind of these cells join together into a single cell. It has a full set of instructions to make life. Eventually, this will become a baby animal or young plant.

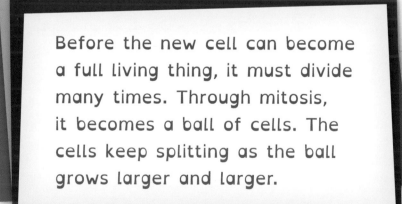

Before the new cell can become a full living thing, it must divide many times. Through mitosis, it becomes a ball of cells. The cells keep splitting as the ball grows larger and larger.

Super Cells

Cells are busy day and night. At this minute, cells in your muscles may be building new muscle. In your stomach, cells could be helping you break down your breakfast. And cells in your blood are probably working hard to keep you healthy. Without cells, life wouldn't be possible!

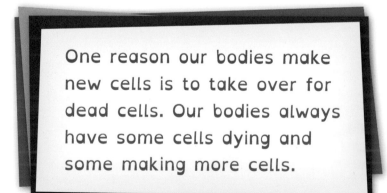

One reason our bodies make new cells is to take over for dead cells. Our bodies always have some cells dying and some making more cells.

Cell Parts

Let's review some of the parts of plant and animal cells.

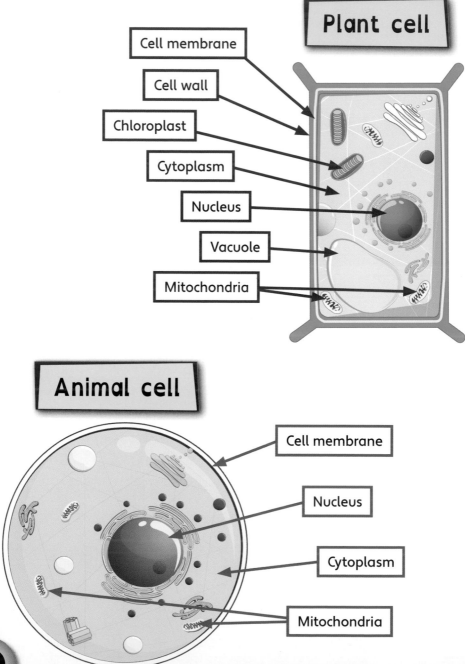

Plant cell

- Cell membrane
- Cell wall
- Chloroplast
- Cytoplasm
- Nucleus
- Vacuole
- Mitochondria

Animal cell

- Cell membrane
- Nucleus
- Cytoplasm
- Mitochondria

★ SilverTips for REVIEW

Review what you've learned. Use the text to help you.

Define key terms

cell membrane

meiosis

mitochondria

mitosis

nucleus

Check for understanding

Name the different parts of plant and animal cells.

What is the job of a cell's nucleus?

How do cells make copies of themselves, and how do they make completely new life?

Think deeper

In what ways do your cells make you different from plants?

★ SilverTips on TEST-TAKING

- **Make a study plan.** Ask your teacher what the test is going to cover. Then, set aside time to study a little bit every day.

- **Read all the questions carefully.** Be sure you know what is being asked.

- **Skip any questions** you don't know how to answer right away. Mark them and come back later if you have time.

Glossary

chloroplasts parts of cells where photosynthesis happens

cytoplasm the thick, liquid part inside a cell

meiosis the process in which cells divide to begin to make a new living thing

membrane a thin layer that forms a barrier at the edge of a cell

mitochondria tiny parts of cells that make energy

mitosis the process of a single cell splitting into two identical cells

multicellular having many cells

nucleus the part of a cell that controls the cell

reproduce to make more of a living thing

unicellular having or being made of a single cell

vacuole a part of a cell that is filled with fluid, often found within a plant cell

Read More

Finan, Catherine C. *The Human Body (X-treme Facts: Science).* Minneapolis: Bearport Publishing Company, 2021.

London, Martha. *Cells (Discover Biology).* Minneapolis: Abdo Publishing, 2022.

McKenzie, Precious. *The Micro World of Animal and Plant Cells (Micro Science).* North Mankato, MN: Capstone Press, 2022.

Learn More Online

1. Go to **www.factsurfer.com** or scan the QR code below.

2. Enter "**Cells**" into the search box.

3. Click on the cover of this book to see a list of websites.

Index

About the Author

Ruth Owen has been writing books for more than 12 years. She lives in Cornwall, England, just minutes from the ocean. Ruth loves to write books about animals and nature.